WITH THE WORD

JOHN

A Bible Study and Devotional Guide
for Groups or Individuals

MennoMedia

Harrisonburg, VA
Waterloo, ON

With the Word: John
Copyright © 2013 by MennoMedia, Harrisonburg, Virginia 22802
    Released simultaneously in Canada by MennoMedia,
    Waterloo, Ontario N2L 6H7. All rights reserved.
International Standard Book Number: 978-0-8361-9695-5
Printed in United States of America
Edited by Ken Beidler, cover and interior design by Merrill R. Miller

Sessions from *Adult Bible Study Teacher* and *Adult Bible Study Student*, along with *Rejoice!* daily devotions, were all used in the writing of *With the Word: John*.

All rights reserved. This publication may not be reproduced, stored in a retrieval system, or transmitted in whole or in part, in any form, by any means, electronic, mechanical, photocopying, recording, or otherwise without prior permission of the copyright owners.

Scripture quotation taken from the Holy Bible, *New Revised Standard Version Bible*, copyright ©1989, Division of Christian Education of the National Council of the Churches of Christ in the United States of America. Used by permission. All rights reserved.
To order or request information, please call 1-800-245-7894 in the U.S. or 1-800-631-6535 in Canada. Or visit www.mennomedia.org.

17 16 15 14 13   10 9 8 7 6 5 4 3 2 1

MennoMedia

Table of contents

Introduction
5

Session format
7

1. The Word was in the beginning (John 1:1-8)
8

2. Christ, the image of God (John 1:9-18)
14

3. God's Word saves (John 3:1-21)
20

4. The Good Shepherd (John 10:1-18)
26

5. To be a servant (John 13:1-20)
32

6. No place like home (John 14:1-14)
38

7. Dawn of a new day (John 20:1-18)
44

8. A new community in Christ (John 20:19-31)
50

Introduction

* *

Welcome to *With the Word*! This exciting series from MennoMedia invites you to draw closer to God by spending time with the Word through Bible study and daily devotions.

Studying John

Who is Jesus? This is a central question in the gospel of John. As a storyteller, John uses details, plots, and characters to help readers understand who Jesus is as God on earth and who Jesus is as Redeemer. John's purpose is to help readers come to belief in Jesus and to claim his significance in their own lives and in the life of the faith community.

The gospel of John has two main sections: chapters 1–12 and chapters 13–20. The first 12 chapters focus on Jesus' public teachings and interactions with a wide variety of people through words and actions. They emphasize belief and unbelief, with belief leading to eternal life. Right from the start, John states that the Word of God became flesh and lived among us. Jesus' earthly credentials are established as we also learn that he is the son of Joseph from Nazareth (1:45).

Chapters 13–20, sometimes called the Book of Glory, tell of the passion of Jesus and his teachings given only to those who believe. This section begins with a farewell message from Jesus to the disciples. It marks private time between Jesus and his followers to prepare them for his upcoming death. Jesus reveals that he is the way to God (14:6), and then he is crucified and resurrected. "Love one another" is John's ethical command from these chapters.

While the first half of the book contains images of light and life, the second half addresses love and costly discipleship. Together, these two parts accomplish the purpose for the book: "But these are written so that you may come to believe that Jesus is the Messiah, the Son of God, and that through believing you may have life in his name" (20:31).

Through the revelation of Jesus, we are provided the gift of salvation.

Session format

In this volume on John, you will find eight sessions for either group or individual use. The easy-to-use format starts with an in-depth Bible study and ends with seven short devotionals designed to be read in the days after the session. Here's a guide to each session:

- **Opening:** The opening of the Bible-study portion calls you into the session through a summary of the text and a few questions for reflection. Before you begin each session, take time to read the text reflectively.
- **For the leader:** These are ideas for how to use the material in a group setting. If using the material individually, omit this section.
- **Understanding God's Word:** This section makes connections between the session's text and today's world.
- **Connecting with God's Word:** This is the heart of the guide; it's the in-depth Bible study that calls you to examine specific parts of the session's text. The writer gives background for a few verses of text, then outlines a series of questions for personal reflection or discussion. These questions always invite you to make connections between the biblical text and your own life.
- **Closing:** The Bible-study portion of the session then closes with a brief time of worship and wrapping up.
- **Devotionals:** Immediately after the sessions you will find seven short devotionals on the session's text. Each devotional starts with a Scripture verse, includes a meditation, and ends with a prayer. Use these seven inspiring devotionals in the days after the session as way to keep the text in your heart and mind.

Spend time *With the Word* today!

1

The Word was in the beginning

JOHN 1:1-8

Opening

Think about times in your life when you eagerly anticipated an event or a person's arrival. What did you do while you waited? What feelings did you have? God sent Jesus, the Word, to dwell among us. How has the story of Jesus' light breaking into the world changed your life? What responses of praise and joy can you add to this anthem of praise in John's gospel?

Understanding God's Word

What is God like? Where is God? What exactly is the relationship between Jesus and God? These questions have been the subject of theological reflection for centuries, beginning in the Scripture texts themselves.

The Jewish and Greek contexts for understanding John's prologue are both important. The Greek term *logos* (word) was familiar to John's audience as a term of philosophical significance. It referred to the rational principle or creative force that permeated the universe and gave it order, stability, and direction. The Greek *logos*, however, was not a personal being as it is in John's prologue.

The Jewish context is also significant for understanding John's description of Jesus as "the Word." "In the beginning" recalls Genesis 1, the story of

For the leader

1. Ask for a volunteer to read John 1:1-8. Suggest to the class that they listen for the word *light* as it appears in the text in different ways. Following the reading, turn out the lights in your classroom and light a candle.

2. In the candlelight, ask members of the class to share how they experienced God's light breaking into the darkness of the world in the past week. Encourage sharing of both personal and global examples.

God speaking the world into being. God's word in the Old Testament makes things happen. It is not only word but also deed. Psalm 33:6 says that God's word created the heavens. "The word of the Lord," received and passed on by the prophets to God's people, is never empty. It creates, judges, and redeems.

The prologue introduces themes and images that appear and reappear throughout the gospel, like colorful threads in an intricately woven tapestry: life, light, truth, glory, belief, rejection. In simple language it proclaims profound truths about the origin and identity of Jesus Christ.

Connecting with God's Word

The Word became flesh

The prologue, or introduction, of John's gospel begins by telling us about Jesus' origins in a way that not only makes clear that Jesus is divine but also praises him with poetic language. Note the intricate poetic structure of the first five verses: John uses step parallelism: the noun used at the end of each clause or sentence becomes the subject of the next. Jesus is the *Logos*, the Word. He did not gain his status by appointment as a *messiah* (in Greek, *christos*, "anointed one"). Rather, as the animating principle in creation, Jesus existed prior to creation. From the story in Genesis, we understand that God works through speaking. Therefore Jesus, the Word, does God's work.

Sometimes the Old Testament and other Jewish writings speak of God's word almost as an independent entity, in a way very similar to how Proverbs 8:22-31 speaks of Wisdom. Isaiah 55:11 says, "So shall my word be that goes out from my mouth; it shall not return to me empty, but it shall accomplish that which I purpose. . . ." In such texts, Word and Wisdom are personifications of aspects of God. This in no way compromised strong Jewish monotheism, for Wisdom and Word were not intermediaries or lesser gods, but intrinsic parts of God's divine identity. They were the creative and revelatory expressions of God's will.

This helps us understand what John's readers would have heard in the prologue. The Word of God was with God from before time. The Word was God's agent in the creation of the world and had been active in carrying out God's will throughout history. The astounding dimension of John's claim is that this Word of God has become flesh and blood and lived among us, making God's glory visible to ordinary people! In coming into the world, he brought life and light to all people. The darkness of the world could not overcome the Word, and so the light continues to shine.

- In ancient times it was easier to believe that Jesus appeared to have flesh than to believe that he came in the flesh. With what view of the flesh does the prologue provide us? What does having a body make possible for Jesus?

- Unlike Matthew and Luke, John's gospel does not have a birth narrative. John tells a different story of Jesus' origin. How does the poetic and theological language of John's prologue add to our understanding of Jesus' beginnings found in the other gospels?

A witness to the light

After an abstract, poetic prologue, the verses that speak about John anchor the Word firmly in history. A real person named John prepared for the coming of the Word. Like the prophets, he was sent from God. His witness was authoritative.

Some scholars believe the story of John interrupted the *Logos* hymn to make clear to the original readers that those who followed John the Baptist were on the wrong track. Within the norms of ancient speeches, this aside serves to compare Jesus with someone whom many in his generation loved and considered righteous. For many years after Jesus' earthly life, John was still more widely known. The fact that John the Baptist witnessed about Jesus shows how much more worthy Jesus was of praise.

- What are some other biblical examples of people whose lives and ministries were connected through this pattern of witness and fulfillment?

- Are there examples in your congregation or in your life of ways that God prepared a way through one person's ministry or presence, leading to a greater realization of God's plan and purpose?

In this gospel, John is not called the Baptist, nor is he the real focus of attention. In fact, the evangelist emphasizes that John was not the light and that Jesus preceded him and surpasses him in rank.

What is Jesus' relationship to John the Baptist? John's mission was to bear witness to the light in order that people might believe through him. In the gospel of John, being a witness is an appropriate and important role to have in relationship to Jesus. John "came as a witness," and he came "to testify to the light."

- Christian witness comes in many forms, through both word and deed. We see modeled in John the Baptist's and Jesus' lives a way of servanthood. Reflect on experiences you have had of genuine and loving Christian witness. What virtues or characteristics do we need to be authentic witnesses of Jesus in our world?

Closing

Sing together "Praise, I Will Praise You, Lord," number 76 in *Hymnal: A Worship Book* (Scottdale, PA: Mennonite Publishing House, 1992), or offer a prayer of praise for the gift of Jesus, the Word who came to bring light and life to each person.

Devotionals

Devotional 1

In the beginning was the Word, and the Word was with God, and the Word was God. —John 1:1

I recently spent an afternoon with a group of Nicaraguan women from a poor, urban neighborhood. I asked them to speak the first ideas that came to them when I said the word *power*. They spontaneously responded with "abuse, exploitation, lacking love, authoritarian, unjust." Looking at the list, they noticed that all the associations were negative.

An imbalance of power gets in the way of a mutual relationship between the powerful and the powerless. Power can force obedience and respect, but power can't call forth love.

Our all-powerful God became all-vulnerable. With the birth of Jesus, God came to us totally empty and powerless in order to call forth our love. God freely chose to dwell among us in emptiness, openness, and vulnerability in order that we may freely choose abundant life. May we celebrate today with grateful hearts as we draw close to the Word made flesh. –*Susan Classen*

All-powerful, all-vulnerable God, you entered our world in human form so that we might freely choose to accept your love. Thank you.

Devotional 2

In him was life, and the life was the light of all people. —John 1:4

One Christmas Eve many years ago, I sat in darkness, nursing our baby daughter and feeling sorry for myself. We were living in Paraguay, where Christmas falls at the hottest time of year. We were also far from our Canadian home. I missed my extended family, along with other things that trigger the Christmas spirit in me: roast turkey, pine trees, and concerts.

After our sons had opened their presents and before everyone went to bed, my husband and I washed and hung a load of diapers. Later, sitting in the dark, I noticed a tiny blinking light. It was a firefly moving across the living-room floor, marking its passage by signals, as if swinging a lantern. I felt as if that creature had come just for me, to remind me of something and to bless me. The firefly reminded me of the real meaning of Christmas. God, the true light, has come and enlightened the darkness of our world. –*Dora Dueck*

Thank you, Lord Jesus Christ, for being the light that enlightens the world and our hearts.

Devotional 3

The light shines in the darkness, and the darkness did not overcome it. —John 1:5

Rembrandt's painting *Head of Christ* shows a face full of grief and love, painted in golden light, just barely emerging from dark, chaotic shadow. It is clear that the glow in the painting shines from within Jesus. But the sadness in Jesus' eyes tells us that he well understands the darkness of pain and death that surrounds him.

The emotions that fuel this world's darkness—anger, fear, greed, lust, power, arrogance, pride—are the human traits that created the cross. When these sins are uppermost in me, they are often invisible to me.

Jesus dramatically models the light for us. And God's Spirit strikes the match that lights up our inner selves with God's love. The light is contagious, sparking from God's Spirit into each believer, from the Creator into our universe, and thus into our beautiful but weary reality. *—Mary Lou Cummings*

May the light of Jesus show on my face and in my heart today. May the light of God's Spirit guide my steps.

Devotional 4

The light shines in the darkness, and the darkness did not overcome it. —John 1:5

I spend more than 40 hours a week in a lockdown hospital: behind clanging doors, intimidating sally ports, security cameras, and razor wire. Sometimes when approaching the buildings, one can hear the screams of angry or despairing patients.

On weekends I travel one hundred miles away from there, walk to the riverbank, and become still. I breathe deeply. I say, "Thank you for this wetness. Thank you for this grass, for these berries and thorns, for these firs, and for this gray sky."

Then I return the hundred miles to the hospital. I am greeted by the excitement of a patient who's had an unexpected phone call from a lost daughter, and by the moist eyes of another who claims he has not been able to cry for 10 years. The Light snagged on the razor wire has not been overcome by the darkness. *—Lani Wright*

Thank you for the Light. And thank you for the night, which is not darkness to you.

Devotional 5

The light shines in the darkness, and the darkness did not overcome it. —John 1:5

I have gone spelunking, or cave exploring, exactly once in my life. It was easy at first, but then I became disoriented in a maze of passageways. In the dark, with tons of rock and dirt between me and the surface, the fear of being trapped with no escape almost overwhelmed me. When I finally saw light from outside streaming into the cave mouth, I was ecstatic with relief and delight.

Darkness is not a benign absence of light but something that threatens to overcome the light. The darkness of sin seeks to entrap, disorient, and frustrate our life and our hope. But because nothing has come into being without Christ, there is nothing that can separate us from the life that is in him. What areas of your life are still gripped by darkness? What would it mean for you to allow Jesus to shine his light in your life? —Matt Hamsher

Free me from the darkness of my sins and fears, Lord Jesus. Lead me out of the depths by the light of your life.

Devotional 6

[John] came as a witness to testify to the light, so that all might believe through him. —John 1:7

My three-year-old grandson enjoys climbing. When he reaches the top of the big slide in the park or conquers the climbing rocks, he tries to get my attention by calling, "Look, Grandma!" If I try to snap a photo to capture his accomplishment, I miss the real action. I have to pay close, direct attention to witness his adventure.

In today's text John the Baptist is the warm-up act before the real Star hits the stage. He gives us the preview show, telling us to listen up, to be on the lookout for the real thing. The life-light is coming, he announces. John's words warn us to pay close attention or we will miss the best part. Those who notice this life-light, who jump onto the stage and join the life-giving chorus, will become "their child-of-God selves" (v. 12 *The Message*). —Elizabeth Raid

God, help me to change my ways of living in response to the life-light Christ brings.

Devotional 7

He himself was not the light; but he came to testify to the light. —John 1:8

Whenever I think of John, I hear a song from the musical *Godspell*, the words of which echo the prophet Isaiah, "Prepare ye the way of the Lord." John's eccentricities are well known—honey and locust eater, clothing made of camel's hair, and a fiery temperament. He was a gifted preacher whose call for repentance drew crowds.

This gospel does not appear to care for any of the colorful detail presented by the other gospels. It simply gets to the point: John is not the light; he comes as a "witness to the light." In this way John the Baptist is a model for each of us. He models how to prepare our hearts for Jesus. He models costly discipleship as he surrenders his own ambitions to become part of God's kingdom. Are there ways today that you can live in the radiance of God's light, and radiate that light to others? —Ken Beidler

God, make us witnesses to your saving love in the world.

Christ, the image of God

JOHN 1:9-18

Opening

Our passage today reminds us that Jesus' message of hope, reconciliation, and love is not always accepted and recognized. Recall a time when you struggled with following God's way. What were the choices you faced? What obstacles did you encounter?

Understanding God's Word

In the second part of the prologue to his gospel, John continues the theme of how Jesus, the divine Word, becomes flesh and blood. Jesus becomes flesh and he "tents" (*skēnoō*) among us. The Greek word for tent, *skēnē*, resembles the Hebrew word for God's tabernacle, *mishkan*. In the story of the exodus, the people see God's glory in the form of a pillar of smoke that enters the tabernacle and dwells with God's people. Later, God's glory dwells within the temple in Jerusalem. Now, we can see God's glory because Jesus makes it manifest, and John makes it appear before our eyes through his storytelling. In the embodied Word, God dwells with humankind in a startling new way.

Yet not everyone accepts the Word/Light that enters the world. This section summarizes the story of Jesus' earthly ministry and the human response

For the leader

1. Bring in several newspapers and church publications (local newspapers, news magazines, *Canadian Mennonite, The Mennonite, Mennonite World Review*, etc.), and distribute them to members of the class.

2. Ask class members to briefly glance through the stories, looking for examples of God's peace, hope, and reconciliation breaking into the world. Also find examples of brokenness and darkness remaining strong.

3. Read John 1:9-18, and then pray for some of the situations in the news.

to the Word/Light when it enters the world. The verb *know* (v. 10) is very important in the gospel of John. Will people recognize Jesus for who he truly is? John loves to tell recognition stories in which people suddenly realize that they are in the presence of someone sent from God. For John, recognizing Jesus is more than understanding what Jesus says about himself. It involves receiving and welcoming him, then making Jesus the center of one's life and imitating him. Whoever does this becomes a child of God.

Connecting with God's Word

The people respond

Rejection and acceptance are important themes throughout John's gospel. Our passage exemplifies three ways in which John speaks of "the world." *First*, the world is a creation of God (v. 3). Since it came into being through the Word, the world cannot be intrinsically evil. *Second*, when the text says that Jesus entered "the world" (v. 9), we see it in a neutral sense as the locus of God's revelation. *Third*, because "the world" did not recognize God's revelation and rejected the Word (v. 10), it stands under God's judgment.

Verse 12 clarifies that to "receive" the Word means to believe in the name of Jesus, and to believe in Jesus means to have life. Those who believe in Jesus will become children of God. Being born of God is not a human activity, like the birth of a child; it is a gift of God.

- Even though most people initially rejected Jesus, a small number accepted him, and that was all that was needed. Later in the gospel, Jesus says that his disciples will do greater signs than those they have witnessed Jesus do. What does this promise of Jesus mean to you? Reflect on how your receiving of Jesus informs your words and actions in the world.

- For Anabaptist Christians, one of the most obvious signs of the world's rejection of Jesus is the prevalence of violence and war. What stories of love and faith challenge the stories of violence that are present in our dominant culture?

The glory of the One and Only

In the ancient world, one's status and identity came from one's father. In the Greek and Roman world, a child had to be claimed by a father in order to receive the father's name and rank. Men of position would often adopt promising younger men as their sons. All the parent's hopes, estate, and name—the things that in the ancient world constituted identity and honor—were handed on to this one child.

In a similar way, John wants us to understand that all those who receive Jesus are adopted by God. With God as our Father, we receive God's name.

We are known as God's children, and we share the name of the real Son. We are Christians.

- The prologue makes it clear that Jesus is divine and inextricably linked with God. Instead of trying to figure out the physics or biology of this divinity, focus upon what the prologue says about receiving Jesus and seeing his glory, the glory that can only be that of God's Son. Is it easiest to see the glory in his miraculous signs? Where do you see the glory when you look at the story of Jesus' life?
- We are beloved daughters and sons of God. How does knowing this help us as we encounter the difficulties and trials of life?

Grace and truth comes
The glory that Jesus inherits is full of grace (*charis*) and truth (*alētheia*). These two words probably refer to two prominent attributes of God described in the Old Testament: *hesed* (loving kindness, or faithfulness) and *emet* (truth, or trustworthiness) (e.g., Hosea 2:20, Psalm 85:10-11). The Old Testament focuses on God's loving faithfulness and the trustworthiness of God's promises. One more aspect of the word *logos* becomes clear. Jesus embodies God's loving kindness and trustworthiness. In Jesus, God's grace and truth are most clearly revealed.

From Jesus the Word, we receive "grace upon grace" in continuous and inexhaustible measure, like the waves on the shore that recede only to be subsumed by bigger waves. Grace and truth from Jesus surpass even the law given through Moses. The prologue concludes the way it began, by affirming the union of the Word with God. Here, however, it uses the relational language of Father and Son that appears in the rest of the gospel.

- In what ways has your congregation experienced God's trustworthy faithfulness over the years?

Closing

Pray together for renewed strength to be witnesses to God's way of "grace upon grace" offered through Jesus. Sing or read "Amazing Grace" (number 143 in *Hymnal: A Worship Book*).

Devotionals

Devotional 1

The true light, which enlightens everyone, was coming into the world. —John 1:9

Christmas is a festival of light. Stroll streets or visit malls, and behold the glitter and glow! Popular programs, publications, and workshops vend expensive soul-transformation secrets. Our world offers dazzling pathways to enlightenment.

True Christmas, though, is priceless: the light of the world is come! John boldly witnesses to the gospel story of Jesus, who calls people to faith, to a divine-human energy connection made real through discipleship.

John's gospel radiates God's priceless yet freely offered love-light. Following this beacon, we find a fascinating life of faith as we walk a daily path of prayer and compassionate service. Christmas sentimentality gives baby Jesus the occasional spotlight—but where is full devotion to the Christ-light? Gospel truth is pure, penetrating life's shadows with limitless love. It liberates the sincere seeker from binding blindness. It illuminates anyone who will walk the disciple's road day by day, carrying that one unfailing candle. –*Doug Schulz*

Lord, deepen in me the power of your living presence as my true life-light.

Devotional 2

He came to what was his own, and his own people did not accept him. —John 1:11

My husband and I have lived in our village community for almost three years, but our work with Mennonite Central Committee frequently takes us to other parts of Costa Rica. When we return from trips, our neighbors enjoy teasing us: "Do I know you? Oh yes, I recognize you from a long time ago."

All is offered in lighthearted jest; nonetheless, these comments sometimes dishearten me in my search for a deeper sense of home. Considering the intensity of my own need to belong, I try to imagine Jesus' reception among his own people of Israel. Like any of us, Jesus must have desired love and acceptance: a sense of home. But instead of being celebrated, he was rejected, persecuted, and crucified. Jesus responded with unfailing mercy and compassion.

What kind of homecoming are we giving Jesus? Do our attitudes, thoughts, and actions acknowledge his loving presence? With grateful hearts, let's welcome him home today. –*Leslie Hawthorne Klingler*

Lord, I open the door of my day and receive you with hospitality and grace.

Devotional 3

But to all who received him, who believed in his name, he gave power to become children of God. —John 1:12

Several of my cousins have not been able to have biological children. It is a difficult and painful reality that many couples face. Some of my family members who have faced infertility have chosen to adopt children.

The theme of adoption runs throughout the Bible and often refers to the way that God has included outsiders. "But when the fullness of the time had come, God sent forth his Son, born of a woman, born under the law, in order to redeem those who were under the law, so that we might receive the adoption as children" (Galatians 4:4-6).

We are all adopted by God. We are all in some way outsiders who need God's grace. It is God's amazing grace that draws us into the family of faith. *—Ken Beidler*

Thank you, God, for your unconditional acceptance that makes us your children.

Devotional 4

And the Word became flesh and lived among us. —John 1:14a

I recently heard about some young, inquisitive children. One of their favorite topics is God. One night, a supper-table conversation made its way to the topic of heaven. One of the children said, "Heaven's pretty scary. God's so big that probably all we could see would be a big toe!"

These children had somehow grasped the bigness of God. The Word, or Jesus, has become God-in-the-flesh. He has lived (or "pitched his tent," as the Greek suggests) here on earth to make God's glory understandable. Whenever we wonder what God is really like, we can turn to Jesus. This same Jesus takes children on his knee and blesses them. The emotion, the forthrightness, the tenderness of Jesus–all of these reveal the character of God. No matter what you face today, remember that Jesus has walked the earth. He knows what it's like to be one of us. You are not alone. *—Aimee Reid*

Giving God, you graced us with Jesus. Draw me close. Wrap me in your presence.

Devotional 5

And the Word became flesh and lived among us, and we have seen his glory, the glory as of a father's only son, full of grace and truth. —John 1:14

I participated in a Thanksgiving camp for international students. One evening was dedicated to home-grown skits from each country. Playing on their reputation for stoicism, the Finns showed slides of how they express joy, wonder, ire, and dismay. Each picture, made to look like the posters that teach preschoolers to name emotions, sported an identical sketch of a bland face. After two or three of these, the audience caught on. My daughter, Mareike, punched me in the shoulder as the laughter increased. "I don't get it! What's the joke?"

Mareike has Asperger's syndrome (an autism spectrum disorder). Her brain doesn't register body language, especially facial expressions. Skills most of us pick up by osmosis–how to greet people in public, how to make friends–we taught step by step to Mareike.

John took the firsthand accounts of the Jesus story and wrapped them in the flesh of inspired commentary in order to send us this message: God spoke Jesus into history so any of us might recognize that the Word has "moved into the neighborhood" (v. 14 *The Message*). –*Lani Wright*

He was the Word that spake it, He took the bread and brake it, And what that Word did make it, I do believe and take it. —John Donne

Devotional 6

And the Word became flesh and lived among us, and we have seen his glory, the glory as of a father's only son, full of grace and truth. —John 1:14

As dawn breaks upon the opening lines of this gospel, it is hard to miss the insistent silhouette of a single verb: *come*. He comes himself, in rough sandaled feet, from that distant home of One who utterly surpasses me. Before any single sign or gesture, before he ever clears his throat to speak, what we glimpse in this unadorned figure rocks our sleepy self-assurance to the marrow. This is what dawns for us here:

> Some have thundered from the mountain ridges. But Jesus came.
>
> Some have winked to us from distant galaxies. But Jesus came.
>
> Some have left us enduring rules and disciplines for life. But Jesus came.
>
> Some sent fiery messages to turn us back from ruin. But Jesus came.
>
> Some have waved a blessing from lofty heights. But Jesus came.
>
> Some have bequeathed to us books of great depth and beauty. But Jesus came.

How can we remain indifferent to such improbable news? Let us rise as a people in grateful acknowledgement of this coming. Let us greet it with amazement and surrender! –*Jonathan Larson*

When Jesus comes, the tempter's power is broken; when Jesus comes, the tears are wiped away . . . For all is changed when Jesus comes to stay. —Oswald Smith

Devotional 7

No one has ever seen God. It is God the only Son, who is close to the Father's heart, who has made him known. —John 1:18

Some time ago, I researched an incident in Mennonite history—an event whose principal players have all passed away. I read about the event in books and articles and began to search through the obituaries of people who had been involved. I wanted to get beyond the mere facts of the case and find human connections. Imagine my delight when I discovered, in one of the obituaries, that the son of one of these persons was someone I knew. Because he was a son and had lived with and known the deceased person, I knew he would be able to make that person "known" to me.

This is the delight of the incarnation—God's coming to us in human form. Jesus knew God! As we contemplate and listen to the words of our Lord this Christmas, let's remember with gratitude that he is the one through whom we know God. –*Dora Dueck*

I'm so glad, Lord, that you know and reveal God's heart to me through your coming, your life, your words.

2 • *Christ, the image of God*

3

God's Word saves

JOHN 3:1-21

Opening

One of the ways that people of faith have carried biblical wisdom into everyday living is through memorizing Scripture texts. What are some of the passages you have memorized? John 3:16 is a text that has been memorized by many Christians. Sing or read "For God So Loved Us" (number 167 in *Hymnal: A Worship Book*).

Understanding God's Word

The Pharisees spent much time memorizing and learning Scripture. Often they appear in a negative light in the Bible—and in our imagination—as opponents of Jesus. Yet they cared deeply about Scripture and its application to daily life.

Nicodemus is a Pharisee. Nicodemus sees the miraculous signs that Jesus performs and infers that he must be from God. He goes to talk to Jesus as a colleague, a fellow rabbi, but he is not prepared to do this publicly. John's gospel is full of one-on-one dialogues in which Jesus quickly moves to the heart of the matter. He engages with his conversation partner in terms that reveal his knowledge of the other person's habits and convictions.

Nicodemus begins by speaking with the confidence of a Pharisee. He thinks he knows what he is talking about. Jesus quickly shows Nicodemus

For the leader

1. Ask one person to read John 3:1-8 and another to read verses 9-15 and 17-21. When the reading comes to verse 16, ask the class to join together in unison.

2. As the Scripture passage is read, ask people to pay attention to words and themes that reoccur in the reading. What is God saying to them and their congregation?

that he still has a great deal to learn. Jesus teaches what he knows from direct experience, rather than from a tradition he has received.

Connecting with God's Word

Born of the Spirit

This passage is dense with wordplays: allusions to Jewish prayers for the resurrection, language for conversion, and probable references to Christian baptism. Early pictures of Christian baptism show the new Christian standing in a basin while water is poured on the head, with the Spirit descending from above in the form of a dove.

Jesus made the point that knowledge of God requires being born again of the Spirit. Some sort of transformative experience beyond Nicodemus's complete comprehension was necessary.

For some denominations, Jesus' words mean that one must be baptized in order to be saved, and so they baptize children as infants. For others, Jesus' words suggest that conversion should be an intense experience in which gifts of the Spirit are manifest. Within the Anabaptist tradition, Jesus' words imply that being part of God's kingdom requires complete obedience. Through that obedience comes true understanding. Since a child's position necessarily requires obedience, baptism should happen at an age when one voluntarily obeys.

Receive the testimony of one lifted up

Jesus used a plural *you* to address Nicodemus as a representative of the Pharisees and a plural *we* to speak as a member of God's heavenly kingdom. The implication was that as long as Nicodemus looked at things from his present perspective, he would not be able to understand Jesus.

When Jesus referred to himself as the Son of Man, he was alluding to the heavenly figure of Daniel 7:13-14, to whom dominion over all people is given. This was not a common messianic title in Jesus' day, but as a Pharisee with a thorough knowledge of Scripture, Nicodemus would have understood the claim that Jesus was making. What Jesus said next surprised Nicodemus, who had no postresurrection hindsight with which to grasp the reference to Jesus' crucifixion. Jesus compared himself to the bronze serpent in Numbers 21:4-9, which Moses lifted up to heal all who were bitten by the poisonous snakes that God had sent as a punishment for their complaining.

- Life for most people in the past, and in most societies today, is a social concept. We exist as a people. Eternal life in John is a reality that we share with God as God's children. In this age of individualism, what has eternal life come to mean?

Not accursed! Loved!

As a Pharisee, Nicodemus would have known Deuteronomy 21:23—that anyone hung on a tree was under a curse. It would have been difficult for him to anticipate that God would send an agent, let alone the Son, to die on a cross. This is why Jesus stressed that his crucifixion would be evidence of God's love for the world and not God's judgment against the world. Jesus later described his willingness to die on behalf of the world as the greatest of loves (John 15:13). Jesus came to make God's glory (God's faithfulness to promises, God's mercy, and God's graciousness) known to the world.

John 3:16 has become the most-quoted verse of the Bible. The Greek wording is difficult to capture in modern English usage. The translation "God so loved the world" might suggest that the quantity of God's love is the issue. But the Greek suggests that the character of God's love is the point. Giving Jesus to the world is how God loves.

- How do you respond when someone asks you, "Have you been born again?" What do you hear when Jesus speaks about being born again?

The light exposes the world's vanity

Jesus anticipated that some would reject the light that he was bringing. The terms he used for their fate could have seemed to contradict what he had just said about not judging the world, but his language made sense within Nicodemus's world, in which a person's status depended upon being honored by others. Jesus was saying that those who did not accept him were worried about losing prestige in the eyes of others. If they stood in the presence of Jesus' true glory, their practices would be shown to be petty (*phaulos*) (v. 20). Those who do God's will are not afraid to receive Jesus and be recognized as God's children, even if the world scoffs at them.

- In this passage we hear Jesus inviting Nicodemus to trust him as a source of wisdom and truth beyond the world's concerns for wealth, prestige, and power. In what ways are you and your congregation being asked to trust more deeply in the abundant life that Jesus offers?

- The verses at the end of this passage have been used to judge and condemn those who do not believe in Jesus. How do you understand these verses?

Closing

Recite or read John 3:16 as a promise for people to take with them into the coming week. Pray for one another that, in times of difficulty and trial, we might find comfort in God's promise of eternal life, here and forever.

Devotionals

Devotional 1

Very truly, I tell you, no one can enter the kingdom of God without being born of water and Spirit. —John 3:5

Physical birth occurs in all kinds of settings and circumstances. Each person's birth represents a unique story and moment in time.

Jesus tells Nicodemus he needs to be born again, or born of the Spirit. Like physical birth, rebirth occurs in a variety of settings with the assistance of a variety of people. In both physical and spiritual birth, some labors are long and difficult, and others are short and easy. Some are unusual, and others routine.

Just as everyone who is living was once born, so everyone who is spiritually alive in Christ has been born again (1 Peter 1:3). Just as we are astonished by the miracle of physical birth, so we stand in awe at the intense miracle of the Spirit of God giving birth to spirit (John 3:6). –*Nancy Heidebrecht Kelley*

Thank you, Lord, for the miracle of rebirth made possible by your grace.

Devotional 2

Very truly, I tell you, we speak of what we know and testify to what we have seen. —John 3:11

The theme of the *With* magazine I was working on was going to be prayer. I phoned a teen who had agreed to talk to me about prayer in her life. Near the end of our conversation Chanita said, "I only say what I know. I only know what I know."

In today's passage Jesus speaks of "what we know, and . . . have seen" (3:11). God loves us. God sent Jesus to give us light during our earthly lives (3:21) and life after death (3:15).

Those who love God and live by God's truth will be vessels through whom God's light shines. –*Carol Duerksen*

God, give me the humility of spirit to allow your light to shine through me, and the courage to give testimony to the amazing power of that experience.

Devotional 3

Just as Moses lifted up the serpent in the wilderness, so must the Son of Man be lifted up, that whoever believes in him may have eternal life. —John 3:14-15

In the Sinai wilderness after the people confessed their rebellion against God, Moses lifted up the bronze serpent. This action brought healing from the effects of their sin and from the punishment of God (Numbers 21:6-9).

Now, when Jesus again speaks of being lifted up, it is in the context of the kind of death that he is to die (John 12:31-33). His being lifted up is not dependent on how many people praise him—or even believe in him. It is a result of his redemptive suffering.

What might it mean to lift Jesus high in your life today? What might communicate to your neighbors, and to those you meet today, that Jesus offers hope and healing to the world? —*Matt Hamsher*

I pray, Lord, that you might be lifted up to bring healing and hope to our hurting world.

* * * * * * * * * * * * * * *

Devotional 4

For God so loved the world that he gave his only Son, so that everyone who believes in him may not perish but may have eternal life. —John 3:16

Watch any sporting event on television, and you'll likely see someone holding a sign that reads "JOHN 3:16." It is probably the most loved, well-known, and frequently quoted verse in the entire Bible. A key phrase in the verse is "who believes in him."

For Anabaptist Christians, belief is more than a onetime decision; it is a way of life. Whether one is holding a JOHN 3:16 sign for a TV audience, raising a Christian family, or otherwise trying diligently to live a Christian life, the call to discipleship is at the heart of who we are as believers. —*Larry Hauder*

Thank you, Lord, for loving the world so much that you sent Jesus into it. Help us to live our belief in him, and thus experience and share eternal life.

* * * * * * * * * * * * * * *

Devotional 5

Light has come into the world. —John 3:1

"Light has come into the world," Jesus teaches. I'm sure if someone would have used this as a slogan for the marketing of the first electric light bulb, it would have been a hit. Today, from a hill overlooking Harrisonburg, Virginia, at night, I can see how that 19th-century invention has spread its light.

If electric light has reached as far as it has over the last 125 years, I can't help but wonder how far Christ's light has spread since he walked the earth 21 centuries ago. Just as there are some parts of the earth that are still without electricity, there are places the message of Christ has not reached. Thank God for the gift of Jesus, and pray that others may find that light. —*Jill Landis*

Jesus Christ, light of the world, may I have the courage to share my light with others today.

Devotional 6

This is the judgment, that the light has come into the world, and people loved darkness rather than light because their deeds were evil. —John 3:19

I have experienced many altar calls. Each time, I've asked: Is God okay with me? Where do I need to change? Without fail, there is darkness hiding in me that needs God's light.

We remain in darkness not because we are ignorant of the light but because we love the shadows. They obscure things we don't do in daylight for fear of exposure. Those things can be as hidden as using tempting Internet sites when everyone else is in bed, or as hideous as shaming a loved one with abuse.

Perhaps the best news of all in this passage is that once we openly admit the worst news—that we love darkness—we are less prone to hide within it.
–Laurie Oswald Robinson

O Lord, please burn away my shadowy false self, and form my true self in the light of Christ's compassion and salvation.

Devotional 7

Those who do what is true come to the light, so that it may be clearly seen that their deeds have been done in God. —John 3:21

At the 2006 Pacific Northwest Mennonite Conference sessions, in a report on restructuring the conference, the consultant said: "You can't get there from here; but you can get there."

When something doesn't work anymore, we often try doing the same thing a little harder. To get new results, we must do new things. God sent us Jesus to show the new way. There were those who saw that in order to get there, they needed to follow the new light of Jesus. They saw the hope of a new life that would be dynamic, inclusive, freeing, and ever reaching forward in faith. With a leap of faith they joined what God was doing in the world. –Bernie Wiebe

God, help us to see that you are doing a new thing through Jesus.

4

The Good Shepherd

JOHN 10:1-18

Opening

Reflect on a time when you felt lost and alone. In what form did help come? How did you experience and receive God's protecting, shepherding love?

Understanding God's Word

In this text Jesus uses an image familiar to rural Palestinians. Sheep were important domestic animals in Palestine. Shepherds were responsible for protecting their flocks and leading them to food and water. In the Old Testament, God is called the Shepherd of Israel (Psalm 23:1; Isaiah 40:11; Ezekiel 34:11-22). Rulers of Israel, who governed on God's behalf, are also depicted as shepherds (2 Samuel 5:2; Numbers 27:15-17) and sometimes as bad shepherds who neglected their flocks (Zechariah 11:4-17; Jeremiah 23:1-4). There is hope that God will send a Davidic shepherd to tend God's flocks with justice and mercy (Micah 5:2-4; Jeremiah 23:4).

In John 10:1-18 Jesus uses this imagery to affirm that he fulfills the scriptural promises of a caring ruler to shepherd Israel. The passage contains two of the seven "I am" statements of Jesus in this gospel. The fact that Jesus speaks of himself both as the gate (door) and as the shepherd is difficult to harmonize. This allegory should not be pressed too hard.

For the leader

1. Has anyone in the class had experience with sheep? If so, allow time for sharing. If not, invite a class member, ahead of time, to do an Internet search about sheep and share the findings.

2. Divide John 10:1-18 into three sections: 1-6, 7-13, and 14-18. Hand out pieces of paper before you read the passage, and invite members to briefly jot down phrases or characteristics that describe a good shepherd.

3. Invite class members to share what they heard.

This text contains contrasts intended to show Jesus as the reliable shepherd over against the false leaders of Israel. Jesus is describing the religious leaders (John 9:40-41; 10:19), with whom his conflict is increasing. Just prior to this discourse, the leaders have failed to be good shepherds to the man born blind. They even drove him away (9:35). What Jesus says about himself stands over against what he sees in his contemporaries.

Connecting with God's Word

Introducing the Good Shepherd
Jesus told a story about a shepherd, a thief, and some smart sheep. John calls this illustration a *paroimia* (proverb) (10:6). A *paroimia* is a proverb or short fable that delivers criticism in an indirect way. In the Mediterranean world in which Jesus lived, proverbs using characters from the agrarian economy were common.

The proverbial picture Jesus painted was very familiar to his audience. Flocks were often owned by a large landowner. The herd was divided into smaller flocks for grazing and tending by hired hands or young sons. Some shepherds tended flocks owned by a number of village families. During the night, sheep from various flocks were driven into a common pen guarded by the gatekeeper, who kept them safe from thieves and predators. In the morning the shepherds would lead out their flocks, each using a distinctive call. In the dry season, shepherds sought pastures in more remote regions and would spend the nights with their sheep, risking attack from wolves. A good shepherd knew the sheep under his care by sight, and gave each a name. Amazingly, the sheep discerned and responded to the voice of their own shepherd. A thief could not herd them away, because they fled strangers.

- In the fourth century when Christian artists first began to paint Jesus as a person, the most popular image was the Good Shepherd. Do you recall seeing images of Jesus as the Good Shepherd?

- Is the image of Jesus as the Good Shepherd still relevant for us today? If so, in what ways do you find this image to be meaningful?

The work of the shepherd
Shepherds lay across the doorway of the sheepfold to prevent sheep from wandering away and hostile intruders from entering. This helps us understand what Jesus may have meant by calling himself both the gate and the shepherd. Jesus is the gate through which one enters to find God and to experience the blessings of salvation. Those who enter by the gate will find pasture, that is, will be nourished and sustained.

When Jesus referred to "all who ever came before me," he was not talking about Abraham, Moses, or the prophets but about those who are called thieves and bandits in verse 1. They were illegitimate leaders seeking their own gain. The contrast in verse 10 captures the key difference between Jesus and the thieves. Their purpose was to harm and destroy; Jesus came to give life in its fullest.

- Doors are often images of invitation and hesitation. Have you ever made a choice to serve God without knowing where the path would lead? How did it turn out? Have you ever played it safe and later regretted a lost opportunity?

- What are the ways that we as God's people are called to both support our leaders and also hold them accountable to be true shepherds of God's people?

I lay down my life

Shepherds and doorkeepers stood at the lowest end of the social scale. At the same time that rulers were called shepherds, the word *shepherd* also could be used as a euphemism for thieves, because shepherds were not always above suspicion. They lived and worked apart from the society of the village or the estate. Jesus accused the Pharisees of acting like the sort of shepherds who saw themselves as only hirelings and not as belonging to the extended household or the community that owned the sheep. Jesus accused the Pharisees of forgetting the people when they were in danger.

In the immediate context of the story, the proverb of the Good Shepherd was directed at the Pharisees as a criticism. But within the broader context of John's gospel, the illustration is about Jesus' role as the Son of God and about the nature of his death. Jesus refers to himself as the Good Shepherd. He knows his people, and as a good shepherd, he will risk his life for them. He is not simply God's employee; he is God's Son. The good son, an obedient son, fulfills his father's will. Earlier in the gospel, Jesus has argued that the work he does is the work he learned by working at his Father's side at creation (5:19-20). Jesus' work is about giving life, but in order to give life to others, he is willing to die. He ends by assuring us that he shares the power of resurrection with God. Dying is not the end of life.

- Jesus longs to shepherd all people. When we are tempted to think that the good news belongs only to us, Jesus says there are "other sheep." Who are the "other sheep" that Jesus refers to at the end of this passage?

Closing

Sing or read the words to "Gentle Shepherd, Come and Lead Us" (number 352 in *Hymnal: A Worship Book*). Pray that God will help bring direction and comfort during times of personal and congregational struggle.

Devotionals

Devotional 1

When he has brought out all his own, he goes ahead of them, and the sheep follow him because they know his voice.
—John 10:4

One of my psychiatrist colleagues purchased a voice-recognition program for his computer to write patient progress notes, because his handwriting was unreadable. He hoped to simply dictate and let the computer print his words. But when I saw what he had to go through to make it practical, I was too intimidated to try it.

In following Christ, the church is like a vast computer in voice-recognition training. We may have installed the software of the Scriptures years ago, but to apply Jesus' words to today's situation still takes hours of rereading and relistening. Yet I know that the only way to ascertain our Shepherd's voice is by paying attention to Christ's words and listening to the Holy Spirit.
–Janet Toews Berg

Good Shepherd, help me to keep hearing your voice and recognizing what you are saying to me.

Devotional 2

The sheep follow him because they know his voice. They will not follow a stranger, but they will run from him. —John 10:4-5

I enjoy watching our son play high-school basketball. The coach calls out plays and shouts instructions to the players as they sprint down the court or defend their basket. Even with the noise of the crowd, the players always seem to be able to hear what their coach is saying.

How do they come to know their coach's voice so well? It is through hours spent in practice: listening to him and putting his instructions into action.

Our coach, our Good Shepherd, is Jesus. The more time we spend listening to him and doing what he teaches us in his Word, the more our hearts will be tuned to hear his voice when life gets intense and other voices are shouting at us. Let us listen for his voice. *–Nancy Heidebrecht Kelley*

Good Shepherd, I want to hear your voice above all others.

Devotional 3

I am the good shepherd. The good shepherd lays down his life for the sheep. —John 10:11

When our son was three, he overheard a conversation between my husband and me that concerned him. We were moving in a few short weeks, and he was unclear about how he fit into the picture. "Who will take care of me?" he asked. We assured him that he would be moving too.

Today's passage from the gospel of John describes Jesus as a good shepherd who would give his life for the sheep in his care. We invest much in our children, in all manner of ways. In the same way that we guide our children, Christ promises to shepherd us through the experiences of life. –*Betti Erb*

Good Shepherd, remind me that I cannot drift beyond the limits of your care.

Devotional 4

I am the good shepherd. The good shepherd lays down his life for the sheep. —John 10:11

My friend Jayne grew up in a large family. The sixth of nine children, she wasn't given much love. She grew up thinking she wasn't worth much. When Jayne had her first child, she couldn't take her eyes or her attention off her precious daughter. She studied her little fingernails and caressed her soft wispy hair. She held her close, accepting the job she'd been given to care for, protect, and nurture this helpless child.

Jayne began to read the Bible through the eyes of her motherhood and to think about God as her own Parent. She knew her Creator must love her even more profoundly than she could love her daughter! Being a mother helped her see herself as a beloved daughter of God. Jesus the Good Shepherd slowly became real to her. –*Sandra Drescher-Lehman*

I pray to you, my Good Shepherd, for the grace to believe how much you love me.

Devotional 5

The hired hand, who is not the shepherd and does not own the sheep, sees the wolf coming and leaves the sheep and runs away. —John 10:12

Jesus' love went beyond a job description. Jesus was saying to his followers, in effect: "I am not simply doing this as a hired hand would do a job. I do what I do because I love you with God's love; I am willing to give up my life for you."

What does this mean for me, as a follower of Jesus? It means going beyond doing good work. My mandate as a psychiatrist is to treat each patient in such a way that I would be able to explain all my actions in a court of law. Jesus challenges me to go beyond that—to love people with God's love. Jesus, not a court or jury, becomes my guiding principle. –*Janet Toews Berg*

Jesus, giving Shepherd, help me today to truly love as you have loved me.

Devotional 6

I am the good shepherd. I know my own and my own know me. —John 10:14

Jesus, along with others in Scripture, compares us with sheep. How fitting! Sheep are not smart. We know how quickly we, on our own, can lose our sense of direction and be led astray.

Psalm 23 reminds us how we need a shepherd to guide us "in right paths" (Psalm 23:3). Sheep are not highly revered among animals. For sheep, life without a shepherd is rather bleak.

I'm learning more and more that in my own efforts and strength, I have no real defense against the dangers around me. I don't need just any shepherd, but one whose voice I recognize and understand. Jesus is that Good Shepherd.
—Bruce Hamsher

When I am tempted to wander off to other pastures, may I remember that the greenest pastures are those where the Good Shepherd has led me.

Devotional 7

I am the good shepherd. I know my own and my own know me. —John 10:14

As many farm folk did, my father and siblings named our cattle. We had a personal connection to all our animals, and many were, to some degree, our friends and companions.

If we know and love animals, how much more must our Good Shepherd value us. In today's well-loved text, this Shepherd knows his sheep by name, and his sheep are on familiar terms with him—at least as far as sheep can be. We know our animal and human friends, but we do not know them as God knows them. God knows all of us better than we know ourselves, sheep that we are, grazing in the pastures of God's love.
—Betti Erb

Thank you, O God, that you know me intimately, and that you care for me.

5

To be a servant

JOHN 13:1-20

Opening

This passage begins at a critical point in Jesus' ministry, when he realizes that the moment has come for him to begin the journey toward the cross and suffering. As he prepares to take this next step, he offers his disciples a spiritual and earthly lesson on what it means to be a servant. Is this a relevant message for us today? How would it change our congregations and our world if people took this lesson on servanthood to heart?

Understanding God's Word

It is ironic that our image of Jesus as servant is drawn from this gospel. Of all four gospels, John reflects the most exalted Christology. John presents Jesus not as a servant but as the Word who is from "the beginning," from outside of space and time. Indeed, John's gospel is structured around this Word's descending from heaven (chapters 1–12) and ascending to the Father (chapters 13–21). The Word does become flesh, but Jesus' feet barely touch the ground. He seems to know everything that will happen to him in the future (13:1). Jesus can read the inner thoughts of people before they speak (2:24-25). Even his dying involves little suffering. There is no struggle in Gethsemane and no strangled, God-forsaken cry from the cross, as in Matthew and Mark.

For the leader

1. Bring a basin of water and a towel. Ahead of time, ask two members of the class to volunteer to wash each other's feet while the passage is read. Have the two volunteers come early to class and begin to wash each other's feet as people enter.

2. Have two persons read the passage (vv. 1-11, vv. 12-20).

3. Ask if anyone would like to share about a time when they participated in the ritual of footwashing. What thoughts come to mind?

John's high Christology is tempered by this very earthly story. Perhaps it is the ultimate irony of this gospel that menial work and servanthood lie at the center of the incarnation. Here Jesus' dirty feet definitely touch the ground!

Connecting with God's Word

Footwashing symbolizes giving one's life on behalf of others

Let's view footwashing as symbolic of something else. Jesus' verbal irony was usually double entendre, in which a word has two meanings: something earthly symbolized something more important in the heavenly world. For example, in John 3 the phrase *born again* actually means being "born from above" by the Spirit.

Most of the time, people understood only the earthly meaning.

Peter was oblivious. In his culture, only servants wash feet, not the *kyrios*, the Lord. "You will never wash my feet," Peter said. But when Jesus explained that if he wouldn't cooperate, Peter couldn't belong to Jesus' community, he wanted a complete bath. Peter did not understand that Jesus' washing their feet symbolized the complete sharing of his life with them, unto death.

- What does the practice of washing feet symbolize for you? Have you found this ritual of the church to be meaningful in your life of faith?

- Women have traditionally been cast in servant roles in the church, as opposed to leadership roles. Does this passage challenge this practice? Do you see examples of how this is changing in your congregation?

Footwashing symbolizes acts of service

Some commentary writers assume that this passage presents two separate meanings for the footwashing. Verses 3-11 present it a symbol for Jesus' death. Since Jesus' death was a unique saving event, disciples cannot emulate it. So another meaning is added in verses 12-20: disciples of Jesus need to wash each other's feet to demonstrate their service to each other.

The Anabaptist understanding unites these two emphases. John 13 humanizes Jesus more than any other passage in this gospel. Not only has Jesus become flesh, but here he also takes the form of a servant, a slave.

John's description roots this event in Palestinian practice. Jesus and his disciples were reclining at supper, but their feet had not been washed before the meal, as was customary in a land of dusty or muddy roads. They had no servants socially lower than themselves. None of them had offered to wash each other's feet. Apparently they preferred to eat with dirty feet rather than lower themselves to this task.

Perhaps Jesus waited to see if any of them would do it, but none offered. Instead, after Judas left, Jesus rose during the meal and did what every servant had to do: He took off his outer garment, which was longer and never worn for manual labor. Underneath was the more practical tunic, which came to the knees. Jesus tied a towel around his waist, poured water in a basin, and proceeded to wash the dirty, callused feet of his disciples and wipe them with the towel.

- Does the ritual of footwashing still symbolize what it was meant to mean? Has it helped you to be a more humble servant?

Peter's reaction to Jesus represents the shame and guilt that the disciples must have felt. Jesus was superior to them; this role reversal should never have happened. But after Jesus explained the symbolic need for such cleansing—to be part of his community—one can imagine that the disciples conceded the point and went back to their dinner.

Jesus made clear his message, "Do you know what I have done to you?" He continues, "So if I, your Lord and Teacher, have washed your feet, you also ought to wash one another's feet. For I have set you an example, that you also should do as I have done to you."

- Jesus suggests that there is no room for class or gender privileges in God's community. From now on, no task is too menial for anyone to perform if you want to be part of God's kingdom. How has the church followed (or failed to follow) Jesus' radical teaching on service?

John differs from the synoptic gospels

Though all Gospels include the Last Supper, only John mentions footwashing. John also omits the sharing of bread and wine as Jesus' body and blood. While Jesus' last meal in the other three gospels is a Passover celebration, in John it comes one day earlier. Since Jesus is presented as the Lamb of God in John 1:29, he must die *before* Passover (13:1), when lambs in Jerusalem are killed.

- How would you compare the symbolism of shared bread and wine with the symbolism of footwashing? Is one stronger than the other? Do they mean the same thing? If not, why do all four gospels omit one or the other ritual?

Closing

Sing or read together "Will You Let Me Be Your Servant" (number 307 in *Hymnal: A Worship Book*). Take time to pray for those in your congregation who are serving the church in different places around the world. Pray for organizations of the church whose mission is service. Pray that each person will have a servant heart this week.

Devotionals

Devotional 1

Having loved his own who were in the world, he loved them to the end. —John 13:1

What does Jesus do in his last days? He has a meal with his closest friends, and he shows love to them in a deep way.

I have never experienced the death of one very close to me, but a number of my friends have described for me their last days with loved ones dying of cancer. In times when death is knocking at the door, spending time with loved ones and expressing love becomes the highest priority. Jesus did nothing different in his last days than he did all of his life. His life was devoted to loving others. If I knew that I would die tomorrow, how would I live? *–Gareth Brandt*

Give us courage, O God, to live and love each day as if it might be our last.

Devotional 2

Jesus said to him, "One who has bathed does not need to wash, except for the feet." —John 13:10

According to John Christopher Thomas, a scholar and pastor, "Footwashing . . . functioned in a variety of ways: as a sign of hospitality, as a means of comfort and hygiene, as a sign of servitude, and as a religious . . . cleansing." Thomas suggests that footwashing played an additional role in early Christian practice. "More than one interpreter has seen in footwashing an allusion to forgiveness of postbaptismal sin."

Baptism represented the bath that provided cleanliness in the new life in Christ. Believers were aware, however, that they continued to sin, even as members of the new community, and that they needed continuing forgiveness. Our churches today also need reminders of God's continuing forgiveness, especially as we share our lives together in fellowship. Again and again God offers us forgiveness. *–Frank Ramirez*

Lord, grant me grace to accept forgiveness and to offer it to others.

Devotional 3

Jesus said... "You are clean, though not all of you." For he knew who was going to betray him. —John 13:10-11

Although the story only tells of the washing of Peter's feet, we assume he washed all of his disciples' feet, including the feet of Judas. The basin that Jesus used to wash the disciples' feet apparently was big enough for all their feet, with all of their filth. Judas would betray him and Peter would deny him later that night. What is our response when it is our turn to put our feet in the basin?

Having our feet washed is a requirement for partnership with Jesus. It means humbling ourselves and being authentic before Jesus with all our imperfections. The basin is big enough for all of us; the water is cleansing, and the hands of Jesus are tender upon our cracked and dirty feet.
–Gareth Brandt

Wash my feet, Lord. Cleanse me and make me whole.

Devotional 4

So if I, your Lord and Teacher, have washed your feet, you also ought to wash one another's feet. —John 13:14

Some congregations in our denomination still wash feet as part of communion services. But in my area, we've left that tradition behind. I don't know if people felt more like servants toward each other when footwashing was practiced, but couldn't we all use a regular dose of something that carries the symbolic weight of footwashing?

What servanthood actually means will be different for each of us. The common denominator will be that sometimes it will feel good, and sometimes it will be downright hard. Jesus gave plenty of examples for us to follow. We just have to tell our bodies, hearts, and minds to kneel down and do it. *–Carol Duerksen*

Servant Leader, I am here now, kneeling with all of my being. Make me a servant, Lord.

Devotional 5

So if I, your Lord and Teacher, have washed your feet, you also ought to wash one another's feet.—John 13:14

I remember my first communion and footwashing service. A few of us young men who had just been baptized entered the room nervously, knowing that whoever we sat beside would be our partner for footwashing. My partner turned out to be a grizzled old farmer with gnarled feet and knobby toes worn by years of hard farm labor. It was a humbling experience, getting down on my knees to wash those feet, but even more so when he struggled to get down on his knees to wash my feet.

Footwashing is the great equalizer (v. 16). No one is greater than another. Age, social status, degrees, income, physical agility, intellectual abilities—all are irrelevant when we bare our feet and wash one another. –*Gareth Brandt*

God, lead me to love and serve those who cross my path today.

Devotional 6

I have set you an example, that you also should do as I have done to you.
—*John 13:15*

It was just after World War II, in Amsterdam. Every Sunday evening Han would attend our Mennonite Central Committee meetings. Little did we know what a powerful influence those meetings would have on Han. Han joined MCC in Amsterdam, helping to resettle refugees and distribute food and material aid. He later worked for MCC in Indonesia, India, Vietnam, and Taiwan. Han was a first-class missionary, always keeping word and deed together.

Jesus' example of serving others by washing their feet has inspired many in history who have courageously kept their walk and their talk together. –*Peter Dyck*

Help us, Lord, to move from word to action, today. May we set good examples for others in our deeds.

Devotional 7

The one who ate my bread has lifted his heel against me. —*John 13:18*

Judas has walked with Jesus for three years, witnessed Jesus' miracles, listened to his teaching, and now shared the Passover meal with Jesus. Why does Judas betray Jesus?

When Jesus chose the twelve to be with him, he knew that there was the possibility of betrayal. In fact, the gospel of Mark has all of the disciples fleeing from the scene when Jesus is arrested (14:50). When the pressure is on, how might we be inclined to look out for ourself ahead of our loved ones?

May we be true to God by being true to those with whom we eat and live in the church and in our families. –*Gareth Brandt*

I will be true to thee, Lord, I will be true to thee. Where thou leadest me I will follow thee. I will be true to thee. —*Leila Naylor Morris*

6

No place like home

JOHN 14:1-14

Opening

In the Bible as well as in our culture, farewell speeches are opportunities for leaders to share their final thoughts and feelings with their followers. Recall a time when you had to leave someone you loved. What feelings did you have? What was good and what was hard about that experience?

Understanding God's Word

John 14 contains Jesus' farewell address to the disciples. Jesus provides them with consolation to ease the sorrow that he knows they will feel at his crucifixion. Jesus' admonition to not "let your hearts be troubled" is not a rebuke but a message of comfort. The disciples of Jesus have good reason to feel troubled. Jesus has just announced that one of them will betray him (13:21) and that Peter will deny him three times (13:37-38). Jesus had also said that he will be leaving them and that they cannot follow where he is going (13:33, 36). Earlier, Jesus himself was "troubled in spirit" at the prospect of one of his own betraying him (13:21). The shadow of death hangs over all of them. To believe or trust in God is one thing; to believe in Jesus amidst talk of denial, departure, and even death is much more difficult. Yet that is what the disciples are to do.

For the leader

1. Give each person a piece of paper and something with which to write. Have them think about what they would choose to say in a farewell speech to their friends and family members.

2. Ask for a volunteer to read Jesus' words (vv.1-4, 6-7, 9-14) and two people to read the questions that Thomas (v. 5) and Philip (v. 8) ask.

Connecting with God's Word

Room in heaven

Jesus used domestic language to help his disciples think of his death as a parting for the good. He began with an image that built on John the Baptist's comparison of Jesus to a bridegroom (3:29). In Jesus' day young couples lived with the husband's extended family. Before the bride entered her father-in-law's house, a place was prepared for her and the children who would follow. In 21:18, when Jesus tells Peter that he will stretch out his hands and another will take him, he seems to be using the same image.

Jesus provided comfort not just for those who were grieving his death but also for all who fear death. Our death is the final journey home.

- Jesus' farewell address responded to the disciples' fear that life would never be the same and that they could not go on by assuring them that the community that he started would continue after his death. When someone who has been the center of your life dies, how have you been able to go on?

- Ernest Becker, an anthropologist, wrote a famous book, *Denial of Death*, in which he argues that much of our existence is built around our avoidance of death. Jesus talks openly about his death and about suffering. How is Jesus' approach instructive for us as we grapple with the subject of human death?

You do know the way!

The disciples frequently interrupt Jesus' farewell speech with questions or comments that make it clear that they do not fully understand. When, at one point, they claim that they finally get it (16:29), we know that they are mistaken. Thomas expresses a fear that many of us have when the people upon whom we rely die: We will be lost without them. Jesus then expresses in adamant terms that Thomas need not worry.

He strings together three "I am" statements. Way, truth, and life are words that point to Jesus' identity. But in the context of the speech, these words also point to Jesus' confidence in his power to save his followers, and his confidence in his followers' knowledge of him. Jesus does not leave us prematurely. What he has said and done, and what the disciples have witnessed, is enough to know who he is—so that we might follow him.

- The threat of death to a loved one can be overwhelming and paralyzing. What are some ways that a Christian community can help those who suffer from grief and loss to experience God's hope and comfort?

- Jesus' words in John 14:6b have become a doctrinal statement about the exclusive role of Christ in salvation. In the context of this story, they are spoken as words of assurance to the disciples. How do you understand these words of Jesus?

Continue to do God's work
Jesus responded to Philip's demand in verse 8 with understandable frustration. As a parent might say, "Do you think I'm made of money?" in response to a teenager's unreasonable demand, Jesus did not ask questions in order to be answered. He wanted to let Philip know that his demand was unreasonable. Then midway through verse 10, we see his frustration giving way to clarification. Jesus explained that we can see God by listening to Jesus, because God is with him. Jesus consistently explained who he is in terms of an ancient economy in which a faithful son works with his father and does his father's work on his father's behalf.

Jesus consoled the disciples by assuring them that his work would not end when he departed to the Father. Those who believe in Jesus receive authority to be children of God. We too can do God's work and represent God through our work. Jesus went so far as to say that the disciples would do greater works than what they had seen him do. The idea that we are able to do God's work is daunting, so Jesus made a promise that whatever we ask in his name he will do.

He added a guarantee to the promise that once more drew from the norms of an ancient Mediterranean economy. When a son did his father's work faithfully, he brought his father honor. When Jesus fulfills our requests, he makes sure that God's work is being done and therefore brings glory to God. When a son conducted his father's affairs, people treated the son with the honor owed to his father. By recognizing that Jesus can answer our requests, we honor God.

- Churches that proclaim the "prosperity gospel" (a teaching that God rewards faith with material wealth and professional success) often cite John 14:14. What did Jesus mean when he said, "You may ask me for anything in my name, and I will do it?"

- Many people who claim to be doing God's work. What are some signs and characteristics that help us discern genuine expressions of God's Spirit at work in the world?

Closing

Sing or read together "He Leadeth Me" (number 599 in *Hymnal: A Worship Book*). Name situations in the world and in your congregation that are in need of prayer. After each prayer request, repeat the words "Jesus says, 'Do not let your heart be troubled. Trust in God; trust also in me.'"

Devotionals

Devotional 1

Do not let your hearts be troubled. Believe in God; believe also in me. —John 14:1

Fear struck the hearts of North Americans midmorning September 11, 2001. As the impact of that day fades, we hope not to forget those caught in the midst of the destruction, along with those who live in the shadow of oppression and war in the Middle East, Asia, and Africa.

A troubling cloud hovered over the disciples as they heard Jesus telling them he was going to leave them. They could not understand what his impending departure and suffering meant. The disciples wanted to remain in a comfortable situation.

I know that feeling. When the status quo is disrupted by loss, when a friend moves away or a death occurs, when the political climate is disrupted, worry and fear crowd into our lives. Jesus' reassuring words calm that uneasiness. *—Jocele T. Meyer*

Jesus, Prince of Peace, in our ups and downs may we trust in you and find your peace.

Devotional 2

In my Father's house there are many dwelling places. If it were not so, would I have told you that I go to prepare a place for you? —John 14:2

On a road trip, most travelers experience a mixture of anticipation and speculation about their accommodations. Recently we have become more comfortable with making online reservations. There is something deeply satisfying about arriving at a destination and hearing the host say, "Your place is ready."

Jesus speaks to his disciples as they agonize about his departure. They are troubled. They are filled with questions and overflowing anxiety, so Jesus tells them, "Do not let your hearts be troubled" (v. 1). He then proceeds to explain why: he is going ahead to prepare a place for them. Not only will their eternal accommodation be prepared, but he will come again and actually take them there himself.

We can enjoy the road trip of life, knowing that Jesus has prepared our destination. Our place is ready. *—Ray Harris*

Thank you, God, for going ahead of us and preparing a place for us for eternity.

Devotional 3

I am the way, and the truth, and the life. No one comes to the Father except through me —John 14:6

The confession that "Jesus is the way" is the fulcrum of our faith. The way to God and heaven is as certain as the One who proclaimed the way during his life, and who died and rose again to open that way. We can trust this way because Jesus is the truth and does not deceive us. We can trust him for eternal life because he lives to impart life. The way to God is open, and it is through Christ that we come to him. Jesus is completely trustworthy. Let us hold our faith with utter confidence and invite others to come to the Way. –Walter Unger

Thank you, Lord, for the certain salvation I have in Christ. Help me to proclaim it and live it today.

Devotional 4

Have I been with you all this time, Philip, and you still do not know me? —John 14:9

I am new to Kentucky and enthusiastic about learning to know the spring flowers blossoming around me. I was pleased, therefore, when a naturalist invited a group for a nature walk. As we walked down the path, I tried to remember the flowers she named and where they grew. During the following week, I returned to the same path. In that familiar setting, I remembered all the flowers she had taught us. Yet when I saw the same flowers in other places, I could not name them!

Jesus comes to us as a friend in ways that are familiar. But Jesus is too big to be contained by one particular context. Knowing Jesus means learning to recognize him when he appears in new and unexpected ways. –Susan Classen

I want to know you, Jesus, in all the freedom and mystery that you are.

Devotional 5

The one who believes in me will also do the works that I do and, in fact, will do greater works than these. —John 14:12

After using this passage as a reading for a funeral, I had an intriguing conversation at the lunch table afterward. One person began to wonder what it would mean if we took Jesus' words seriously—that those who believe in him will do "greater works" than those of Jesus.

A medical student who had just completed her training wondered what it would mean for her to go beyond the numerous examples of healing in Jesus' ministry. How could she bring comfort and hope through her practice of medicine?

That day I was empowered by the fact that Jesus' disciples, along with his later followers, would see Christ's work and life as a beginning rather than an end to the greater work of God. –Doug Snyder

Spirit of Jesus, empower us to do more than we can ever hope or imagine.

Devotional 6

If you love me, you will obey what I command. —John 14:15

Christian faith spread quickly throughout the Roman Empire precisely because of the practical obedience of the early Christians. The language of love spoke volumes in the harsh Roman world of the second century, and it does so in our world too. Jesus tells us that verbal expressions of love for him do not prove our devotion. Obedience does. Words are not the passport into the kingdom. Jesus demonstrated the language of love by being willing to do God's will. That obedience led him from the cradle to the cross.

What better way to demonstrate the language of love than by visiting a lonely or sick neighbor or giving practical aid to someone in need? This is the language everyone understands. *–Walter Unger*

Lord, show me this day how I can demonstrate the language of love to someone in need.

Devotional 7

You know [the Spirit of truth] because he abides with you, and he will be in you. —John 14:17

In Jan Karon's book, *At Home in Mitford*, a series of things mysteriously disappear from the Episcopal Church where Father Tim pastors. A homeless man is finally discovered to be living in the church attic. The man discovers his need for Christ after hearing Father Tim's sermons and requests baptism. At a jail-cell service, the police chief tells Tim, "This feller's had me bawling a time or two." Father Tim responds, "The Holy Spirit tenderizes the heart."

I think that is a wonderful way of expressing one of the roles of the Holy Spirit in our lives. We may be praying for loved ones who need God but find it too hard to believe that God even exists, let alone that Jesus is one with God (v. 9). At such times we need to leave it to the Holy Spirit–the Advocate–to "tenderize the heart." *–Melodie Davis*

Where I have rough edges and a hardened spirit, O Lord, tenderize my heart this day.

7

Dawn of a new day

Acts 9:32-43

Opening

John's resurrection account illustrates our reluctance to believe what we do not think is possible. He does not narrate the actual resurrection, only the evidence that the resurrection has occurred. He focuses on the dramatic turn of emotions from grief to joy, fear to peace, cynical doubt to exuberant belief. Have we become so lost in grief at the suffering of this world that we are not prepared for the joy of the resurrection? Do we resist hope?

Understanding the Word

The Easter accounts in the Gospels differ somewhat in details and casts of characters. No doubt each Christian community cherished truths about the resurrection story that they especially wished to preserve. This seems particularly true for the version of this story preserved in John's gospel.

Mary Magdalene figures prominently in all the gospels as a witness to Jesus' death and resurrection. John describes her as coming to Jesus' tomb "while it was still dark." Since other gospel accounts imply that the sun had risen, we can speculate that John's gospel, where darkness and light are such prominent themes, saves the coming of light until there is belief in Jesus' resurrection.

Discovering that the stone is removed, Mary Magdalene jumps immediately to the conclusion that Jesus' body has been stolen. She runs and reports this to Peter and "the other disciple, the one Jesus loved."

For the leader

1. Read the story of the disciples at the empty tomb in John 20:1-18.

2. Ask whom people identify with the most in John's account of the resurrection story: Mary Magdalene, Peter, or the beloved disciple. Why?

Connecting with God's Word

Gone!

John uses darkness to signify people's failure to recognize that Jesus is the light. Mary's coming while it is still dark points to the depth of her grief and her desperation to honor Jesus in death. Women of her day would not come to such a desolate place alone while it was still night. The sight of the stone rolled away from the tomb set off a chain reaction. Leaping to the wrong conclusion, Mary, and then Peter and another disciple, ran at a speed that matched the frantic state of their emotions. When Mary used the plural, "We do not know where they have laid him," her words became an invitation to the disciples to help her find Jesus' body.

- The presence of four gospel accounts of Jesus adds depth and meaning to our understanding of faith. Which account of the resurrection are you most drawn to?
- The important role of Mary Magdalene in the resurrection accounts as a witness suggests the importance of women in Jesus' life and ministry. Are there women that have played key roles in nurturing your faith?

The evidence

Some readers take the beloved disciple's ability to overtake Peter as a symbol of the superiority of his witness. But when he saw Jesus' linens, he waited to enter the tomb, perhaps in recognition of Peter's seniority.

We see the evidence of Jesus' resurrection, piece by piece, just as Peter saw it. The linens were lying in a way that could have been the result of someone letting them fall when lifting Jesus' body in haste. Then Peter saw a piece of evidence that should have pointed him in another direction: Jesus' head cloth, the kerchief that had been wound around his head to keep his mouth closed. It was "rolled up in a place by itself." No grave robber would have taken such care. Yet Peter failed to recognize this sign that Jesus had arisen.

- Failure to recognize signs of the Spirit's work is part of our journey of faith. The resurrection accounts truthfully and honestly show us that followers of Jesus do not always get it right away. When have you failed to see God's transformative work in your life?
- What is the most important evidence for you of Jesus' resurrection? How has Jesus transformed your life?

Seeing and believing

Tradition has often identified the author of this gospel as John the son of Zebedee, but the gospel refers to him only as "the disciple whom Jesus loved." What we know about him is that he is the eyewitness source for the fourth gospel (21:24) and likely the founder of a Christian community for which his testimony was authoritative. Why the race to the tomb, and why is the winner reported?

Raymond Brown points out that every time the beloved disciple is mentioned, it is in comparison with Peter, and each time Peter is one-upped. Brown suggests that the "community of the beloved disciple" was one that recognized Peter's authority, but they wanted to assert a different kind of authority for their own founder based on loving and being loved by Jesus. Thus the "other disciple" wins the race, and although Peter enters first and sees, the beloved disciple sees and believes.

The significance of the grave clothes being folded neatly and separately may be in contrast to the story of Lazarus, who came out of the grave bound by his grave clothes (John 11:44). Lazarus was merely resuscitated and would die again. Jesus has been transformed into a glorified resurrection body and lives eternally.

- Today, just as in the early church, we have competing visions for who holds authority and power within the church. What do you think of the assertion by biblical scholars that John's resurrection account is shaped by an early Christian community's loyalty to a particular disciple?

- Does this trouble you or help you understand the way that John tells the resurrection story?

The beloved disciple believes
Throughout the gospel of John, the beloved disciple appears as a reserved, quiet disciple. He trails behind Peter as a bystander to the conversation (21:20). He did display some courage when he followed Jesus at his arrest, but he did not yet display the sort of bold speech that he must have come to habitually display as the source for the gospel. John 20:9 suggests that he hadn't yet put all the pieces together. He needed to see Jesus in the flesh, just as the other disciples did.

- Each disciple's development of faith in Jesus is different. When you think of your own journey of faith and the way you have come to know Jesus, do you identify more with Peter or John?

Closing

Say or read together the song "In the Bulb There Is a Flower" (number 614 in *Hymnal: A Worship Book*). Look for signs of God's resurrection hope, and pray that you will experience the power of new life this week.

Devotionals

Devotional 1

Mary Magdalene came to the tomb and saw that the stone had been removed from the tomb. —John 20:1

I had been so proud of keeping the hummingbird feeder up all winter and watching "my" birds every day. Then spring arrived, and I became busy, not tending the feeder or even caring that I did not see hummingbirds. On Good Friday and Saturday, I saw no hummingbirds. Now it was Easter morning, and I felt no inspiration for the day. I stared out at the rain and my empty feeder. Once I thought I saw a flutter but dismissed it as wishful thinking. When in the gathering daylight I saw that tiny bird sitting at the feeder and drinking, I became ecstatic. I felt as though I had been given a second chance.

Today as I relive the account of the resurrection, I accept it as a gift to me. God has given me a second chance.
–Janet Toews Berg

God of new beginnings, I worship you today as I hear again the story of Jesus' resurrection.

Devotional 2

Then the other disciple . . . saw and believed; for as yet they did not understand the scripture, that he must rise from the dead. —John 20:8-9

Growing up on a farm in Pennsylvania, we extended winter daylight in the chicken coop to encourage egg laying. One of my jobs was to go turn out the barn light about 9:00 p.m. so the chickens could get some sleep. It was really dark—and really scary—between the house and the barn. I felt fear in my body. Hairs prickled on the back of my neck; my skin was clammy.

As Peter and the other disciple did, we often understand something in our bodies before our brains categorize it or name it. When Peter and the other disciple saw the empty wrappings, they felt a "yes" in their bodies even before they could register and understand the Scripture that "he must rise from the dead." –Lani Wright

Resurrected Lord, help me to believe in you with all my heart.

Devotional 3

They said to her, "Woman, why are you weeping?"—John 20:13

While shopping I met a young girl who had gotten lost. She turned every way, looking from aisle to aisle with increasing panic. I approached to tell her that the best thing to do would be to stay still and trust her parents to find her. Just then, the mother appeared from around the corner and swept the girl away.

Some commentaries suggest that Jesus appeared to Mary first because she needed him the most. Who knows? But the words with which I had hoped to console that little girl in the store seem to apply to Mary and to us: "Just stay still and Jesus will come to you." In our most difficult moments, he is alive and present. He calls us by name and comforts us. *–Helen J. Tellez*

Risen Lord, thank you that the comfort you gave Mary is the same comfort you offer to us today.

Devotional 4

Why are you weeping? —John 20:15

On March 28, 2006, my sister Karen died after a battle with cancer. By the time she was diagnosed only seven months earlier, the doctors said the cancer was already too far advanced to be operable and gave her only a few months to live. Karen's twin sister, Carol, told me that the night before she died, Karen came to her in a kind of night vision and assured her she would be okay. Karen didn't speak, but she smiled at Carol, turned, and walked away along a path.

On the morning she came to attend to Jesus' tomb, Mary Magdalene was distraught to find it empty. Jesus came to her, not just as a vision but in his real presence, and spoke her name. *–Gordon Houser*

Lord, open my eyes and ears to see and hear your presence and receive your comfort.

Devotional 5

Jesus said to her, "Mary!" She turned and said to him in Hebrew, "Rabbouni!" (which means Teacher). —John 20:16

When a child is born, parents study name books, talk to friends, or consult older family members to find a name that means something to them and will wear well for their child. In some cultures, naming comes later, after parents and community know the child better. The process takes on special significance because the name must represent the child's character and role in the community's life.

Mary heard her name when Jesus called her. There was no other voice like that of Jesus, the one she knew as Lord and teacher.

Jesus' calling of her name drew Mary from her sadness to a state of recognition and response.

In our suffering the risen Lord calls us each by name. *—Elizabeth Raid*

Lord, thank you for standing beside us and calling our names.

❋ ❋ ❋ ❋ ❋ ❋ ❋ ❋ ❋ ❋ ❋ ❋ ❋ ❋ ❋

Devotional 6

Jesus said to [Mary], "Woman, why are you weeping? Whom are you looking for?"... Jesus said to her, "Mary!" —John 20:15-16

For over three years my friend and her husband prayed for a child. Now with a newly adopted son in her arms, she tells me that she thanks God for answering their prayers—not in the way she expected but in the way God knew was most life giving.

When Mary encounters Jesus, she fails to recognize him. While we cannot predict how Jesus will appear to us or anticipate the details of his work among us, we know that he is fulfilling his promises more lovingly and perfectly than we can comprehend.
—Leslie Hawthorne Klingler

Jesus, you are alive!... I hear you calling me by my name!

❋ ❋ ❋ ❋ ❋ ❋ ❋ ❋ ❋ ❋ ❋ ❋ ❋ ❋ ❋

Devotional 7

Jesus said to her, "Do not hold on to me, because I have not yet ascended to the Father." —John 20:17

Imagine yourself in the garden with Mary, in sorrow, and suddenly Jesus appears. What things about Jesus do you want to hold on to? How must you let go? We can understand Mary wanting Jesus to remain as she knew him. But that cannot happen, Jesus tells her. He has to ascend to his heavenly Father, and a whole new world is dawning. As we celebrate the new world introduced by Jesus' resurrection, let us not cling to conceptions of Jesus that are too comfortable. Let us allow him to challenge us to move on in our walk of faith, receiving whatever newness God wants to bring.
—Gordon Houser

I want to hold on to you, Jesus. Help me let you go and walk the road you want me to walk.

8

A new community in Christ

JOHN 20:19-31

Opening

John's resurrection account emphasizes how Jesus dispels fear and gives peace. The peace Jesus gives offers forgiveness that makes it possible to stand in close relationship to him. What emotions do you imagine you will feel when you see Jesus face to face?

Understanding God's Word

In the passage leading up to our study today in John 20:11-18, Mary arrives at the tomb early Sunday morning. She is stunned to see the stone removed and the tomb empty. She reports this to Peter and the disciple that Jesus loved.

Mary stands weeping before the tomb. Even the two angels in white cannot comfort her. When Jesus speaks to her, she recognizes him and reports to the disciples: "I have seen the Lord."

There are many ways to focus on the risen Christ at Easter—worship, art, reading Scripture. Easter facilitates meditation on what Christ did for us in his death and resurrection. Why is this important? The end of John 20 tells us that the signs that Jesus did are written so "that you may believe" and thus "have life" (v. 31). We stand before the cross and the empty tomb at Easter

For the leader

1. Have a sign outside the door of your room with instructions to enter the room in silence. Turn out the lights in your room, or keep them dimly lit.

2. Invite people into the room, and explain the situation that the disciples were in. They were uncertain, afraid of enemies, and grieving the loss of Jesus as their leader and friend.

3. Give the volunteer a small light to read John 20:19-31, emphasizing Jesus' words "Peace be with you" in verses 19, 21, and 26.

so that we might believe in Christ—the Priest-King and the Word of God—who is wise, caring, and glorious. May we come to trust Christ in a new way this Easter and thus "have life in his name" (John 20:31).

Connecting with God's Word

The sign of peace

The disciples stayed hunkered down in their hiding place. Perhaps they thought that if Lazarus' resurrection had led to Jesus' death (11:45-53), Jesus' resurrection would lead to a death warrant for all of them. Their encounter with the resurrected Lord put their fear side by side with the peace that Jesus offered.

Jesus' words "peace be with you" and the gesture of holding out his hands served to dispel their grief. He had not come to punish them for their failures or shortcomings. He had fulfilled his promise to them (14:27; 16:20-24). Now they could experience Mary's joy.

Jesus' peace is much more than the absence of strife or fear. It is a shared well-being, a sense of abundance from which we can share with others. Jesus' words were soon followed by the gift of the Spirit that emboldened the disciples to become witnesses to Jesus' grace. Based on John 20:29, some readers treat the resurrection appearances as unnecessary to faith, and they criticize the disciples for failing to believe without seeing Jesus.

- The disciples' fears in the face of uncertainty are experienced in our own journey of faith. Jesus' presence overcomes that fear. First John 4:18 says, "Perfect love casts out fear." In what ways have you or your congregation experienced the peace of the risen Jesus that "casts out fear"?

- Centuries later, we rely on hearing the disciples' witness to the resurrection. How is it different for us than it was for the first disciples?

Jesus brings peace, not a sword

Some pieces of Jewish literature in Jesus' time pictured God's Messiah coming with a sword in his hand with which to avenge God (e.g., Dead Sea Scrolls, Damascus Document 19:9-11). Jesus held out his hand and showed his wounds, and but he did not say, "Look what they did to me," as if to provoke the need for retribution. He said, "Peace." In doing so, he dispelled any anger that the disciples might have felt. Consider for a moment how extraordinary it is that the story of the early church is not one of revenge. It is rather a story of widening circles of witness and inclusion of outsiders.

- How is Jesus' message of reconciling love being lived out in your life and the life of your congregation?

Doubting Thomas

While the other gospels each mentions Thomas only once, John mentions him seven times and gives us the further information that he's a twin. We may consider doubt a weak faith, but elsewhere in John's gospel, Thomas says he is willing to go with Jesus and die with him (11:16). Jesus treated him gently. He accepted his doubt and his need to touch his side. Then he put this need into perspective when he said, "Blessed are those who have not seen and yet have come to believe."

When we are prone toward unbelief, Jesus comes to us and says, "Peace be with you." He does not dismiss our questions, yet in the end we are called to believe and to act in faith that Jesus is with us through the Holy Spirit.

- Faith and doubt are often contrasted in the Christian life. Yet most of us struggle with some moments of doubt. Can doubt lead to a stronger faith in the long run?

- When Jesus asked Thomas to touch his side he wanted his disciples to remember how he had suffered and also to know without a doubt that he is real. What does it mean for our life of faith to believe that Jesus really did suffer and that he is fully human like us?

Jesus gives the gift of the Holy Spirit before Pentecost

Within this story the promise was fulfilled that Jesus' death would bring eternal life and make possible the coming of the Holy Spirit. Jesus offered peace, purpose (sending), and power (the Holy Spirit). John's imagery links the coming of the Holy Spirit to creation and the gift of God's animating spirit (Genesis 2:7).

- In what ways does receiving the breath of Jesus enable you to breathe forgiveness and peace to others? In what specific ways does forgiveness shape the church's identity?

Closing

Take a few minutes to reflect on what you have learned from the study of John. Take some paper and write down some reflections:

- What will you remember from your study of the book of John?

- What is one new learning that you will carry with you?

Pray for strength and wisdom to continue to live out the gospel's call to follow Jesus and bear the fruit of justice and mercy in the world. Share the peace of Christ by saying, "The peace of Christ be with you."

Devotionals

Devotional 1

Jesus came and stood among them and said, "Peace be with you." —John 20:19

Jesus did us a tremendous favor in choosing folks who so often mirror our own frailties. They argue, get jealous, make mistakes, are slow to catch on, deny they know him, and even betray him. Here, these followers are just plain scared and shaking behind a locked door. Yet these doubting and fearful disciples go on to witness to what they have seen and heard and know.

Like the disciples, we all have our doubts. Yet we move ahead with faith, growing and believing as the Holy Spirit works in our lives and the lives of those around us. *—Melodie M. Davis*

Lord Jesus, we give you our fears and our doubts as we strive to move ahead in faith and trust.

Devotional 2

Jesus came and stood among them and said, "Peace be with you." —John 20:19

I can identify with the disciples. There are days when I feel scared and overwhelmed. Then Jesus appears and says, "Peace be with you." Often my skeptical response is "Sure, right."

But when I stop and listen, I realize that I do have peace. It's just hard to remember this in my fear. I think of a favorite verse or song. A friend calls or sends me a note. I see a smiling child or a beautiful flower. I decide to journal about my fears. Things aren't any different. The problems aren't solved. I just know that I have peace and somehow that is enough. *—Karen Jantzi*

Give thanks to Jesus for bringing peace to you. Think of ways you can bring peace to people in your life.

Devotional 3

Jesus said to them again, "Peace be with you!" —John 20:21

At a family gathering last summer, those of us who had lived through World War II and other military conflicts shared our experiences as conscientious objectors to war. We were challenged as we heard stories of nonresistance in times of extreme patriotism. Some had performed alternative duty in Civilian Public Service in the United States, while others had done relief work in war-torn areas. Our group agreed that peace is a way of life that must be lived every day.

The reading today recounts two appearances of Jesus to his disciples after his resurrection. Three times he says, "Peace be with you," both as a greeting and as a blessing. Peace is the longing of all in our world today. The peace of Christ is not the result of force or of violence but of love, gentleness, and generosity. *–Edna Krueger Dyck*

Lord Jesus, make us channels of your peace.

Devotional 4

[Jesus] showed them his hands and his side. Then the disciples rejoiced when they saw the Lord. —John 20:20

There's no richer joy than being in contact with the living God! Our world today has so many people who no longer could be called, to borrow a term from C. S. Lewis, "supernaturalists." C. S. Lewis himself once viewed trust in the supernatural as "an illicit dram" (a desperate alcoholic's secret sip of something). But Lewis, an honest seeker touched by the truth of the resurrection story, became a believer. As those disciples did, he saw the Lord!

The Easter proclamation of Christ's life—present to us, for us, and in us—is the heart of Christian faith. It's refreshing truth, a joyful vision for every day! *–Doug Schulz*

Lord, I want to know the joy of resurrection life. Touch my unbelief with your living presence.

Devotional 5

He showed them his hands . . . he breathed on them and said to them, "Receive the Holy Spirit." —John 20:20, 22

Some years ago a student wanted help to know for sure that God was in her life. I gave her the following exercise: Begin by placing your palms up as a symbol of your desire to turn over all your concerns to God. Pray, "Lord, I give my cares to you." Now turn those palms down and invite God to take those cares. Let go! Open your palms again and invite Jesus to breathe his Holy Spirit into you.

About 10 days later she came by my office all excited. She had been able to turn her cares and concerns over to Jesus. Months later, the student came to me again—discouraged that she no longer felt at peace.

Jesus' appearance to his disciples so soon after his resurrection was only a beginning. I told her Jesus' disciples grow step by step. —*Bernie Wiebe*

Thank you, dear Jesus, for patiently making yourself known to us more and more fully.

Devotional 6

If you forgive the sins of any, they are forgiven them; if your retain the sins of any, they are retained. —John 20:23

Suddenly Jesus stood among them, speaking peace. Jesus commissioned the disciples to go out and do what he has done: forgive. The power to forgive is the very life of God, who is love. Forgiveness is the ultimate act of Christ.

The disciples had seen the worst that humans—including themselves!—were capable of doing. The joy of Jesus' sudden, incredible presence showed what God had done with their guilt and weakness. Now they had the power and responsibility to offer others what Jesus had offered them—God's loving forgiveness, the essence of the gospel. —*Mary Raber*

Holy Spirit, remind us of our responsibility to carry forgiveness to others, and of our authority and power to do so.

Devotional 7

Jesus said to him, "Have you believed because you have seen me? Blessed are those who have not seen and yet have come to believe." —John 20:29

I tend to believe everything anyone tells me with a straight face. I've had to learn that not everything people present as the truth is necessarily so.

Thomas had that healthy dose of skepticism. Sometimes we dismiss him negatively as "doubting Thomas" for insisting on seeing the risen Savior himself. His desire for an eyewitness experience, however, shows his humanity. Jesus did not rebuke Thomas. Rather, he offered the physical proof that Thomas sought and needed, and then he praised those whose doubt turns to faith. Having seen and felt for himself, Thomas became the first to address Jesus as both Lord and God. Doubting Thomas paved the way for us to take our own doubts to Jesus. —*Amy Dueckman*

God, increase my faith so that, with Thomas, I may encounter you as "my Lord and my God."